I0832248

white noir

robert fleming

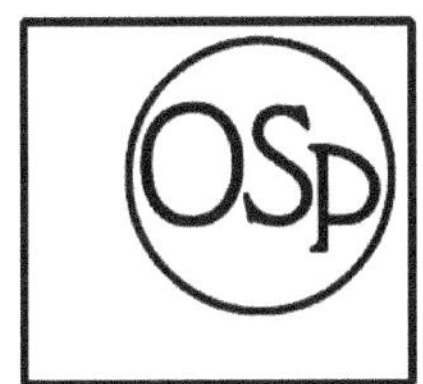

Published by Old Scratch Press, an imprint of Devil's Party Press, LLC.

ISBN: 978-1-957224-18-3

Printed in the United States of America.

FIND US AT
oldscratchpress.com
devilspartypress.com

Acknowledgements

My first language is French and my second is English. I am grateful for my mother Sybil and English teacher, Ms. Berger, who recognized in 1975 (grade 7, 12-years-old) that I wrote English sentences like French and helped me learn how to write English sentences like English.

My Brandeis college poetry teacher, Denise Levertov, who in 1983 encouraged me.

Gail Braune Comorat, a poetry free-write leader for the Rehoboth Beach Writers Guild, who leads a Monday workshop where I wrote/drew first drafts of +-33% of the works in this book.

JoAnn Balingit, a teacher who taught two workshops of visual poetry at the Woodlawn Library in DE where I learned about visual poetry and created drafts of some of the works in this book.

Members of critique groups who gave me feedback, especially David Siller, at the Poetry Academy of DC, and Gregory Foster at Spectrum.

Carol Grem who inspired me to create the work Murder by sending me videos of crows.

I am grateful to the editors and staff of the following journals in which versions of my works first appeared:

Spectrum: *blanche à noir, noir à blanche, 3-line stooges, ÷ time*
Four Feathers Press: *ozone repair trial #2001: band aid, ozone repair trial #10022: Elmers glue, spatula, norman bates journal*
Medusa's kitchen: *moon evolves, satan's commandments, playground earth, housing futures*
Synchronized Chaos: *Alexa can miracles exist?, tree ring research proposal, tree ring share, tabula rasa*
Dumpster Fire Press: *can't get rid of them, city black out*
Blazevox: *United Nations finds pedestrian driver switch = peace, person black out*
Read Green Books: *trigger finger, survival of the fittest hand*
Failed Haiku: *murder*
Cajun Mutt Press: *patience only for my last line*
National Beat Poetry Foundation: *five male singing voices grid*
Fevers of the Mind: *return to the garden*
Impspired: *we were before waring*

Contents

Foreword

What a freaking weirdo.

That's what I thought when I first saw Robert Fleming. He was at the Friday night garage poets open mic zoom call, hosted by Jeff Taylor. Jeff was talking,

Robert butted in, letting Jeff know that he created a Halloween flyer for the open mic and asked Jeff to share the screen. The image that appeared took me by surprise. It was a picture of a garage, but there was also a chainsaw and other weapons, decapitated heads, and blood. There was a strange silence over the call.

Later that night, Robert read some of his poems and explained that he was a word artist. I had never heard of such a thing, but I realized that I was witnessing it.

Flipping through *white noir*, you have never seen or read anything like this. Through images and words you will see and think things that you wish you never did or ever will again. Get on Robert's Mr. Toad's wild ride, a journey through one of the most original minds. You will be blessed by the curse of what keeps Robert up at night and makes him chuckle through the day.

Matt Wall
Publisher, Poetic Anarchy Press
Los Angeles
August 2023

white noir

white noir
robert fleming

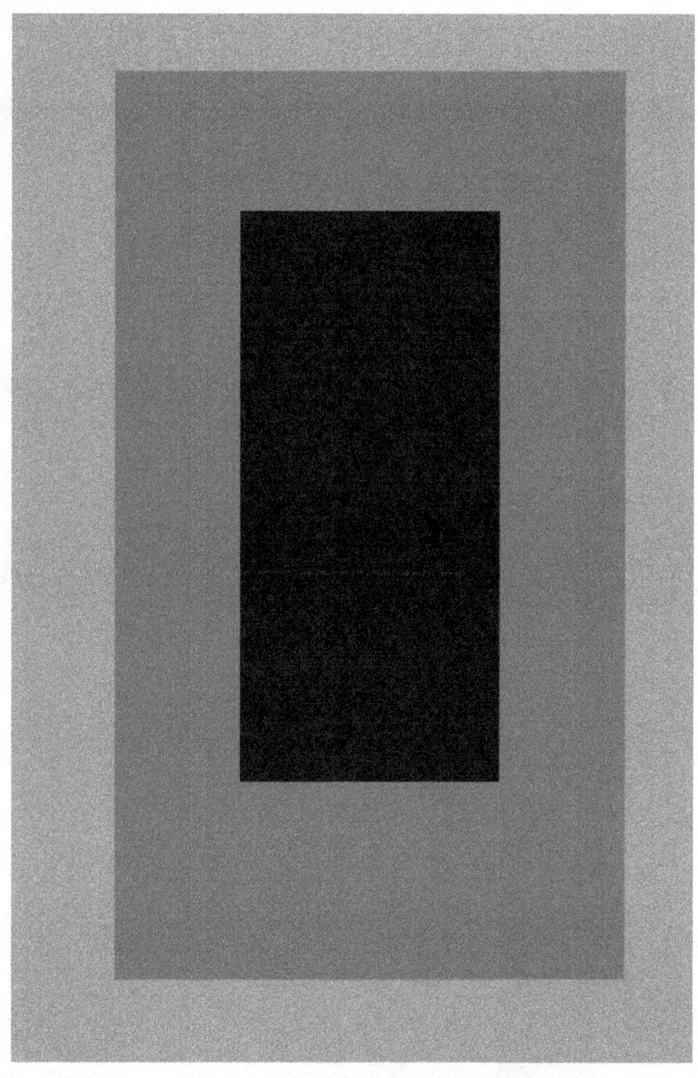

blanche à noir

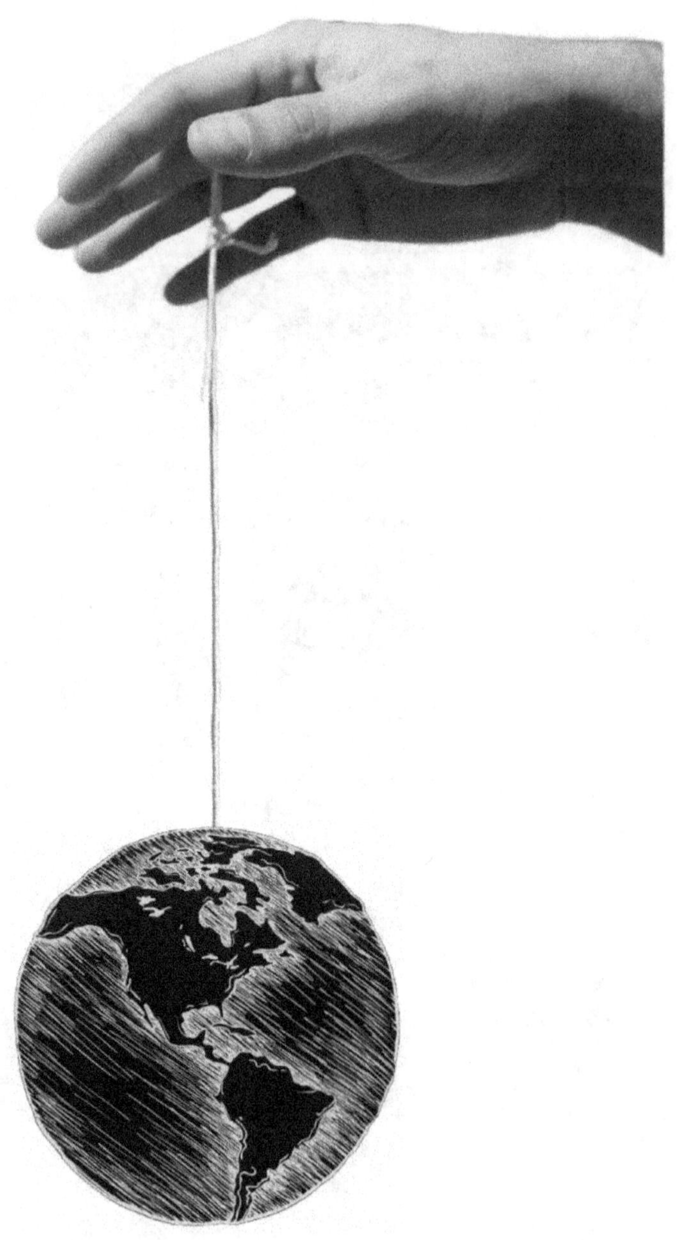

playground earth

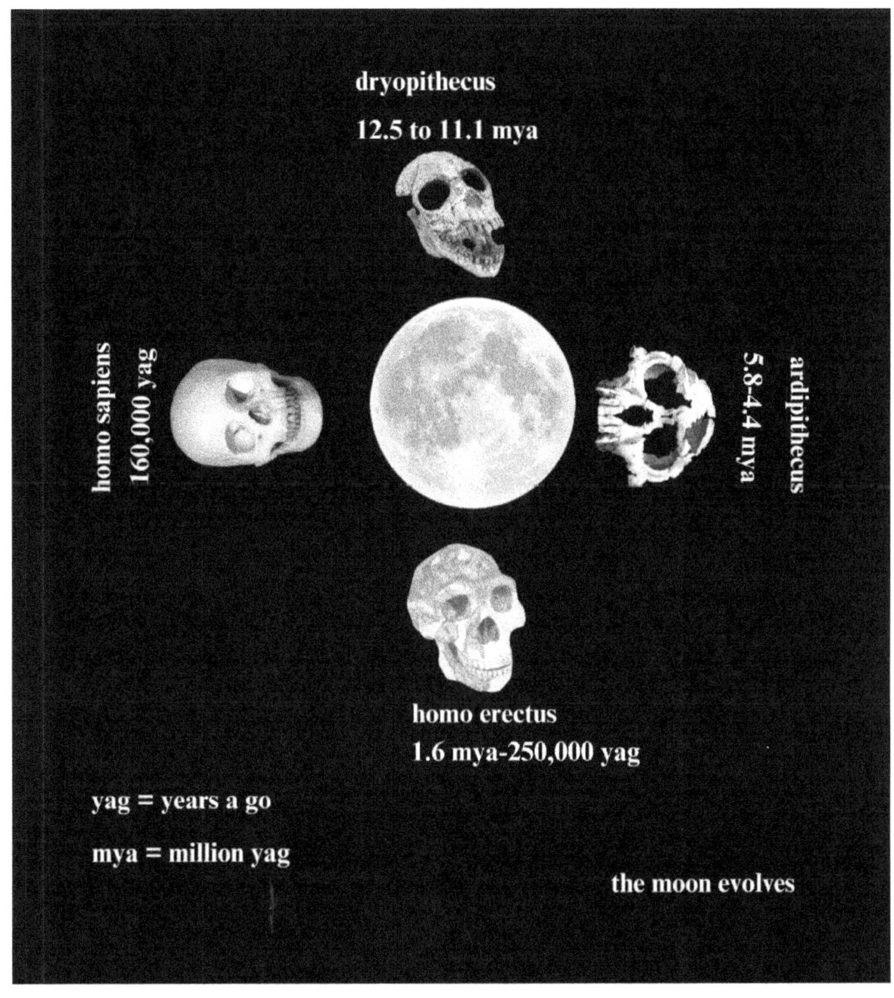
dryopithecus
12.5 to 11.1 mya
homo sapiens
160,000 yag
ardipithecus
5.8-4.4 mya
homo erectus
1.6 mya-250,000 yag
yag = years a go
mya = million yag
the moon evolves

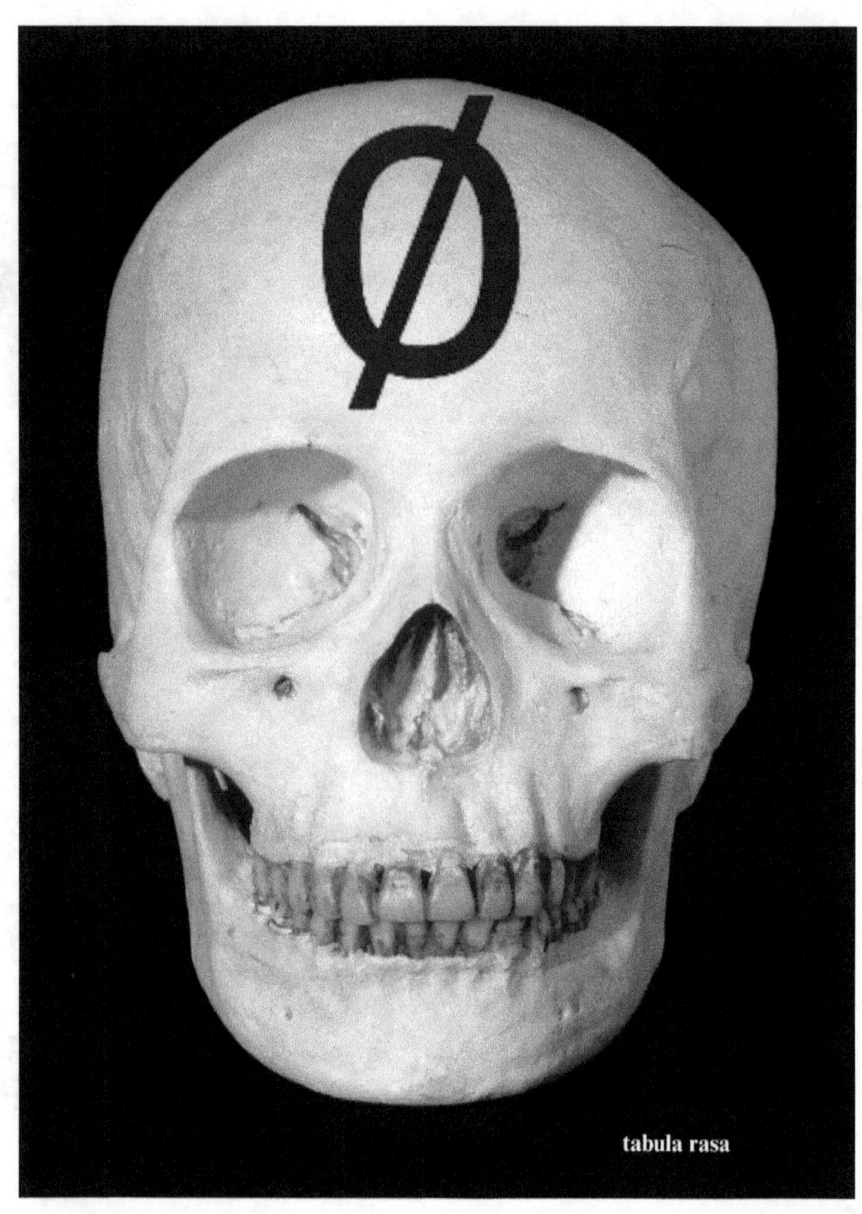
Ø
tabula rasa

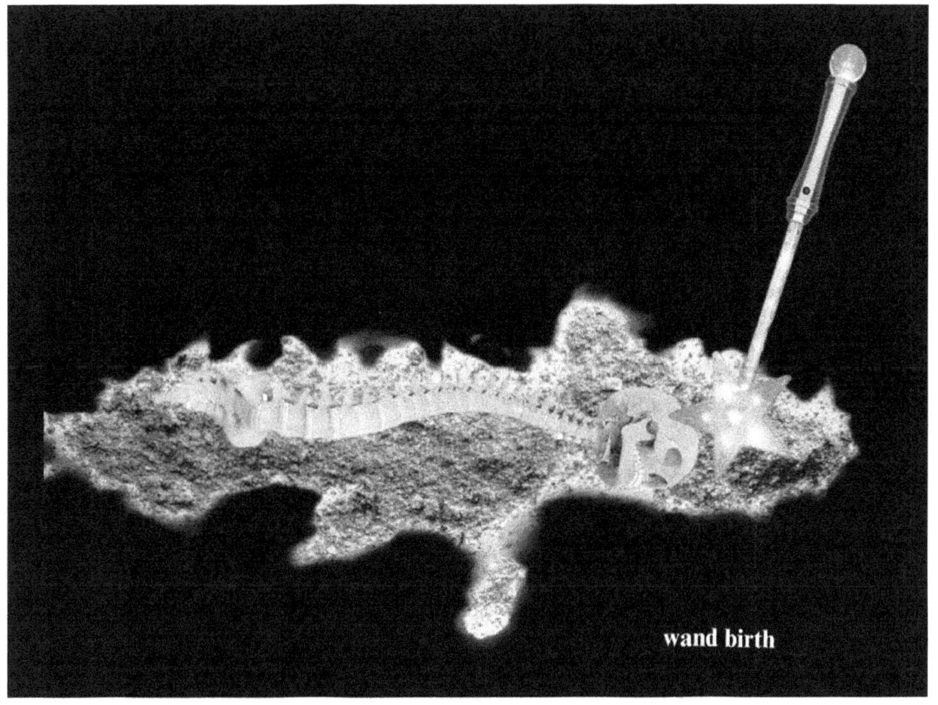
wand birth

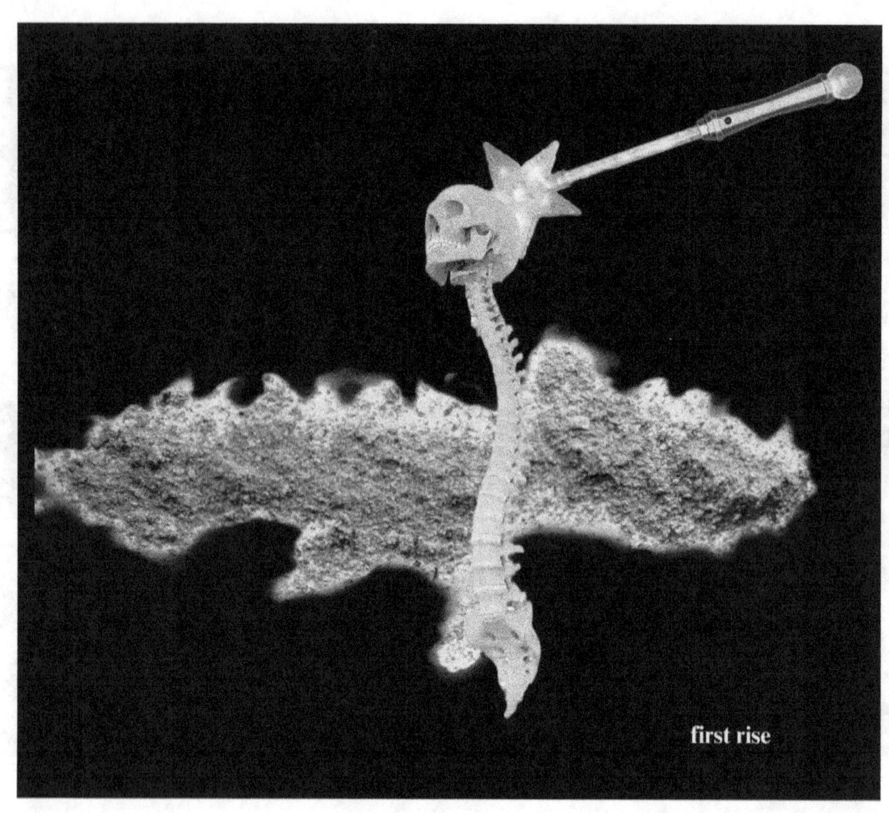
first rise

LIFE
IF E
FE
E
HTEAD
H TEA
TH A
H T
H
E
FE
I FE

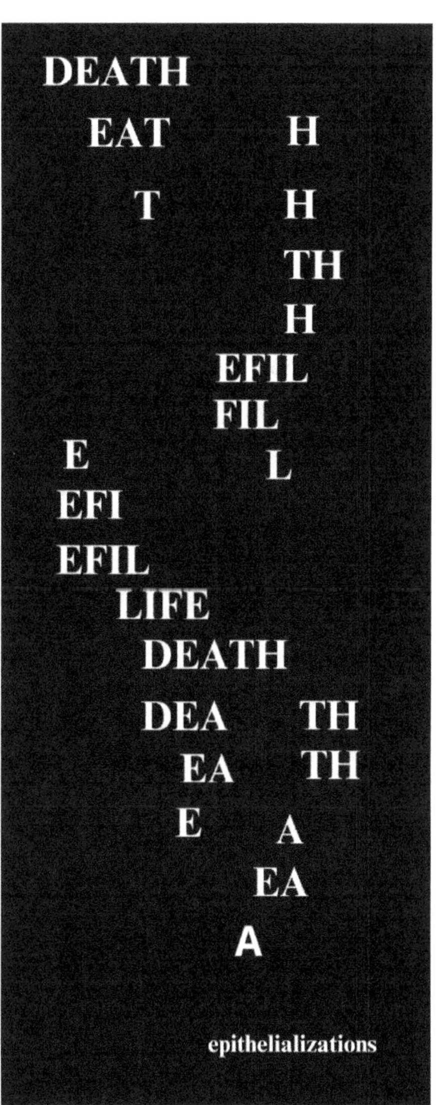

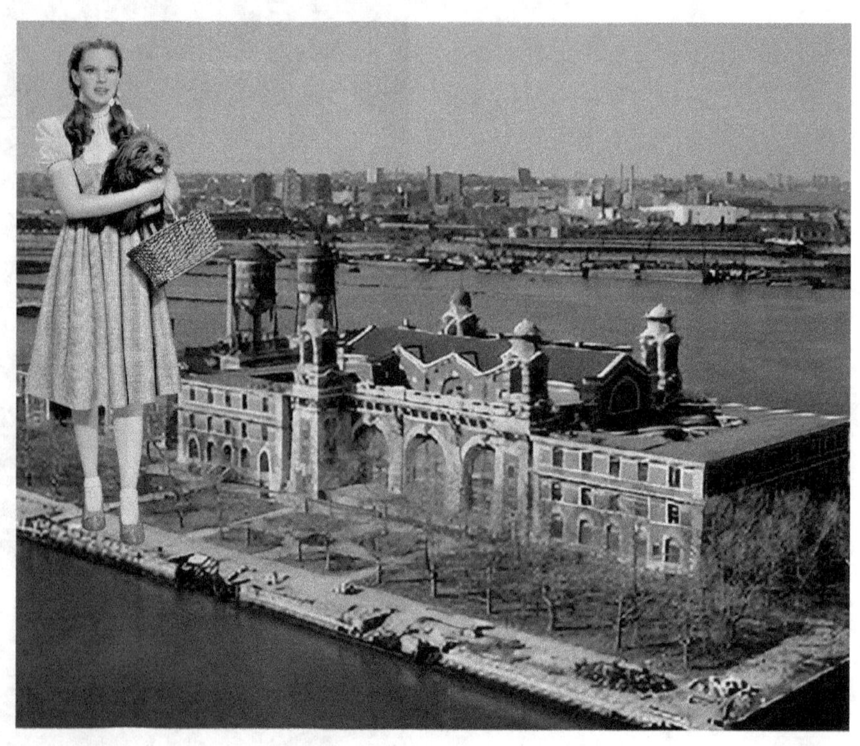

the wizard gave them a country

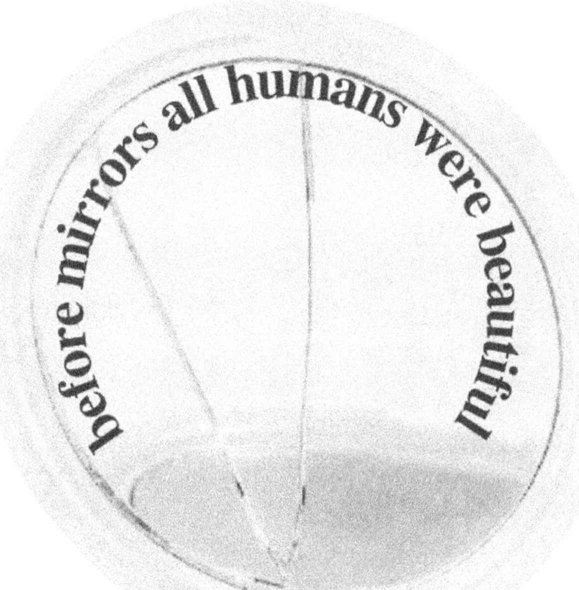

**The object of desire
is ugly when
a mirror reflects**

New York city exhibitionist and Hoboken New Jersey voyeur on the thirty-second story across the Hudson River

ten pm	mp net
blinds	niatruc
raise	llup
undress	pirts
towel	teehs
binoculars	sraluconib
naked	edun
masturbate	etabrutsam
climax	xamilc
sdnilb	curtain
lower	pull

white noir

robert fleming

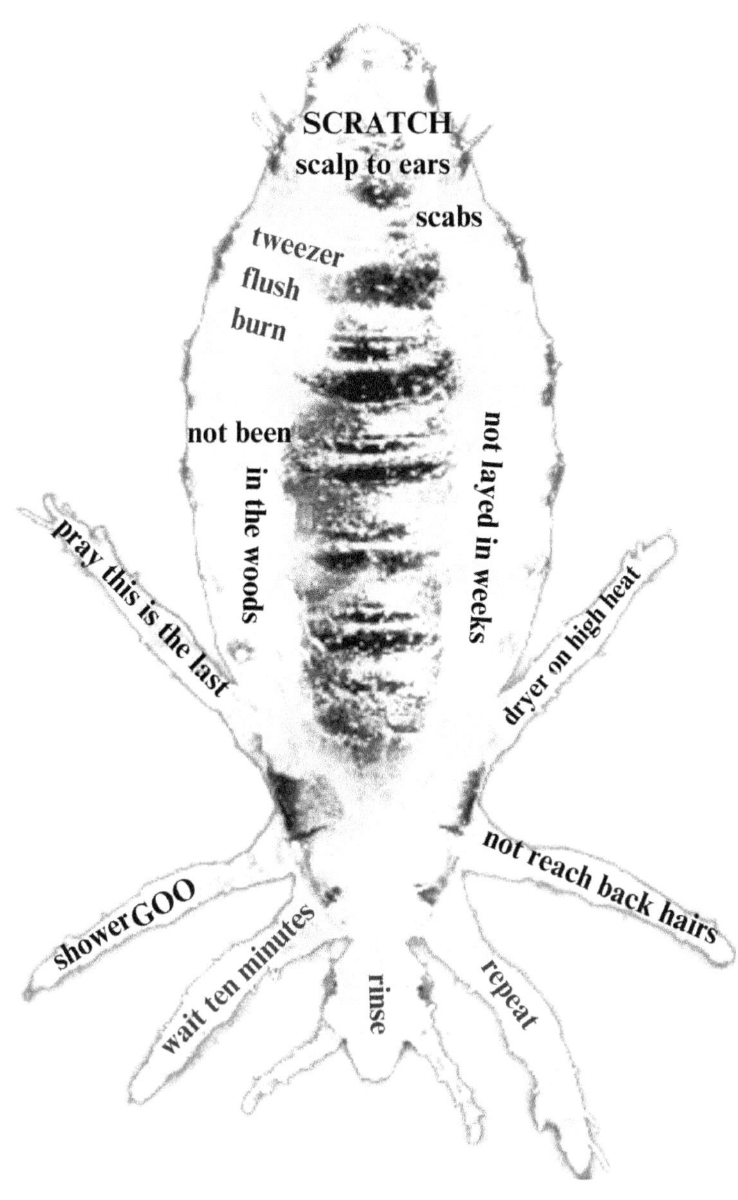

can't get rid of them

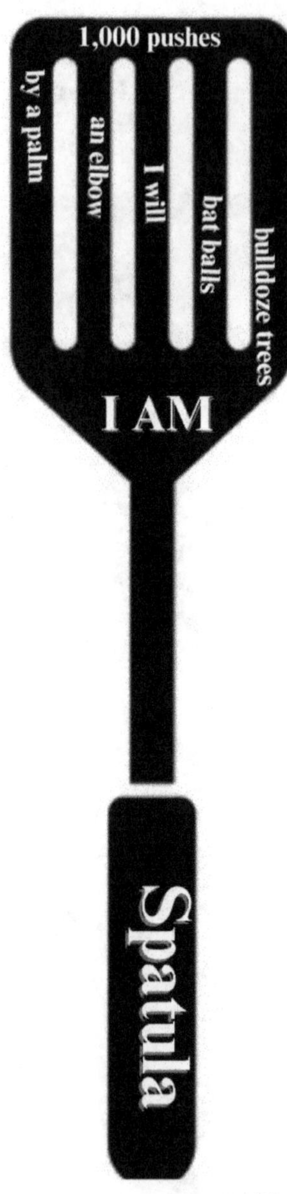
1,000 pushes
by a palm
an elbow
I will
bat balls
bulldoze trees
I AM
Spatula

spatula

3-line Stooges

Larry

girth 2 mirth
2 much girth shortens mirth
2 little mirth longens girth

Moe

cud 2 dud
the cow chewed cud, i chewed milk duds
milk duds mashed in 2 cow cud

Curly

lipstick 2 tick
reapplied green lipstick as the bomb ticked
tickled ur nipples with neon lipstick

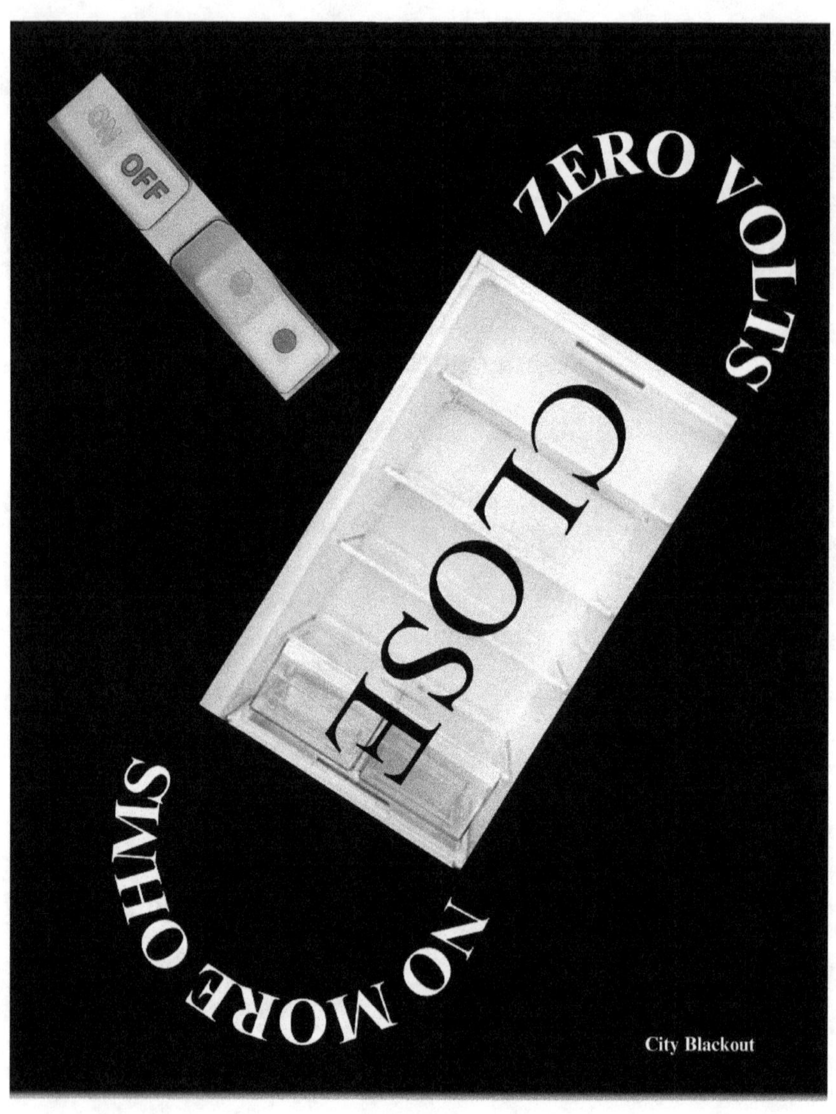
ON
OFF
ZERO VOLTS
CLOSE
NO MORE OHMS
City Blackout

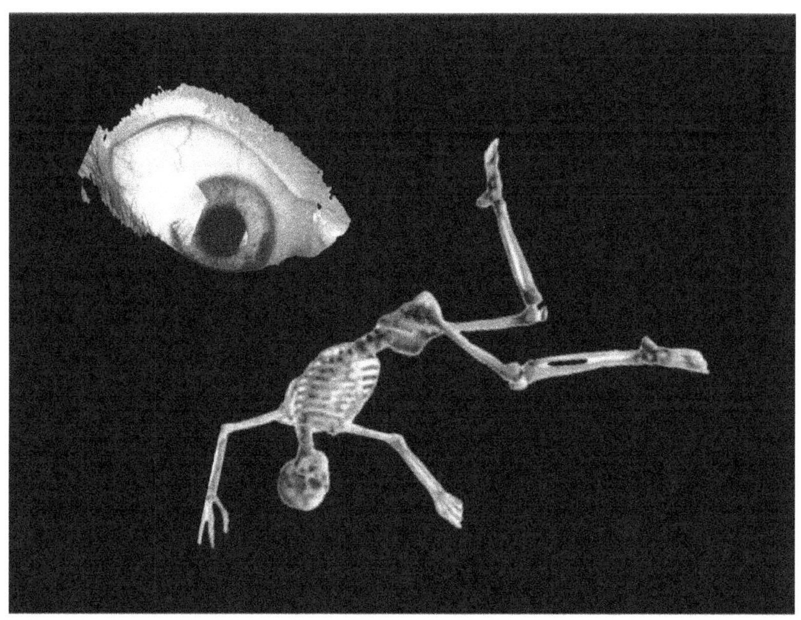

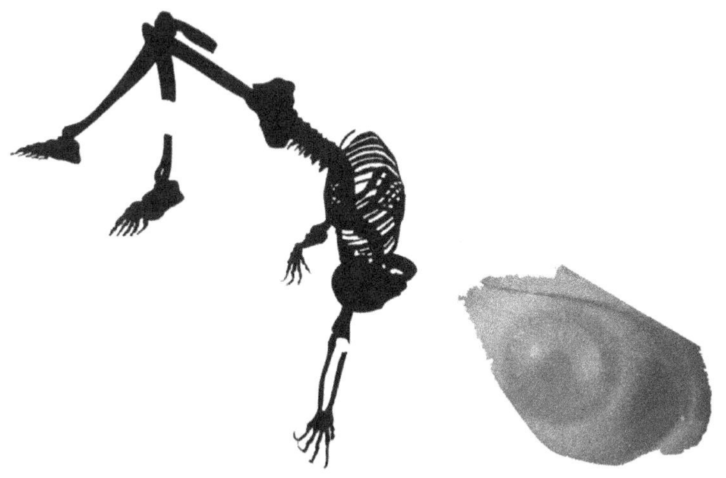

Human Blackout

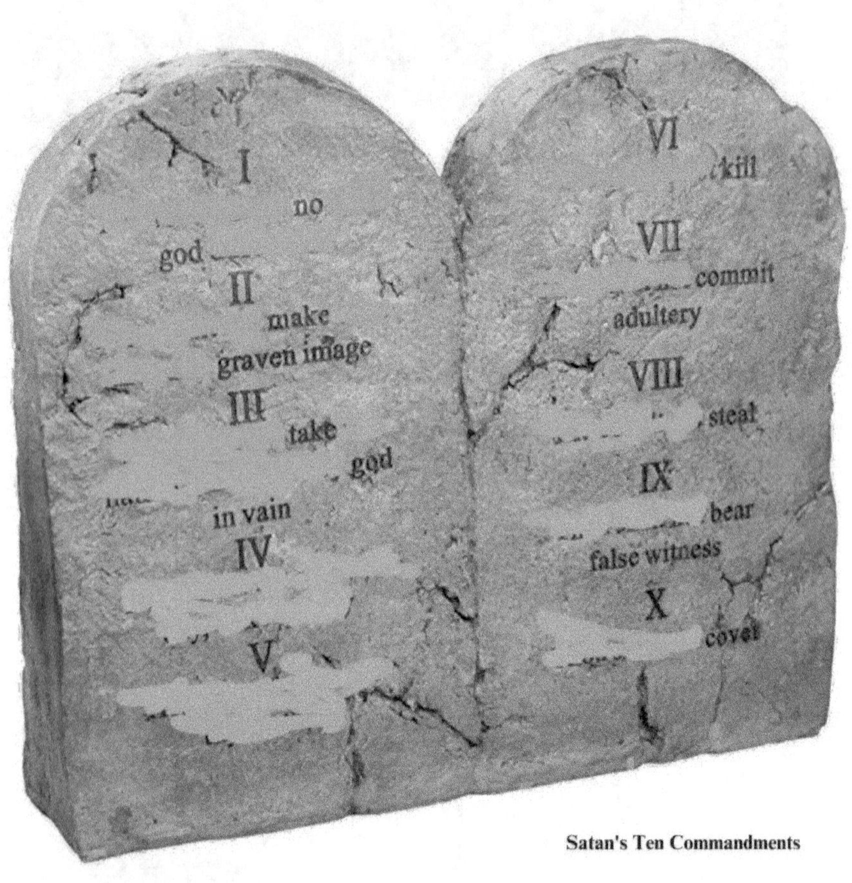

Satan's Ten Commandments

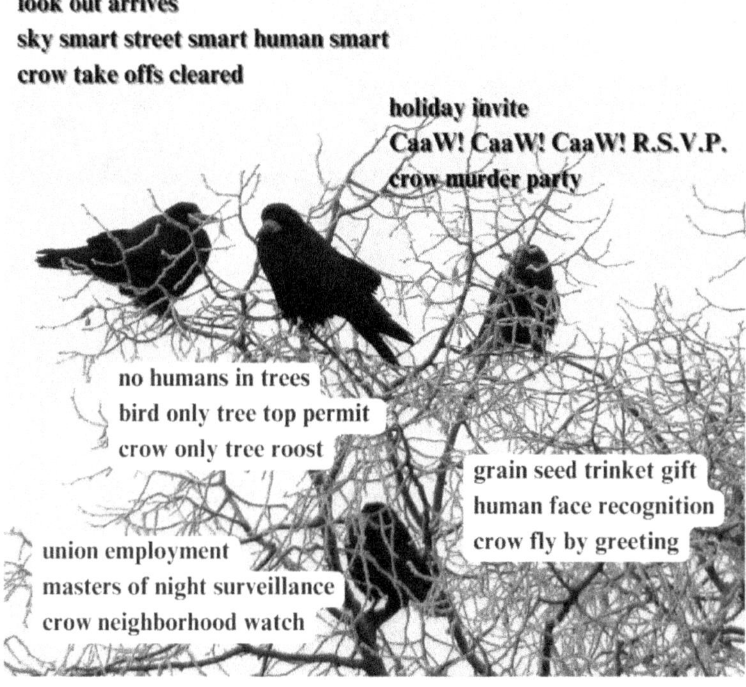
look out arrives
sky smart street smart human smart
crow take offs cleared
holiday invite
CaaW! CaaW! CaaW! R.S.V.P.
crow murder party
no humans in trees
bird only tree top permit
crow only tree roost
grain seed trinket gift
human face recognition
crow fly by greeting
union employment
masters of night surveillance
crow neighborhood watch

murder

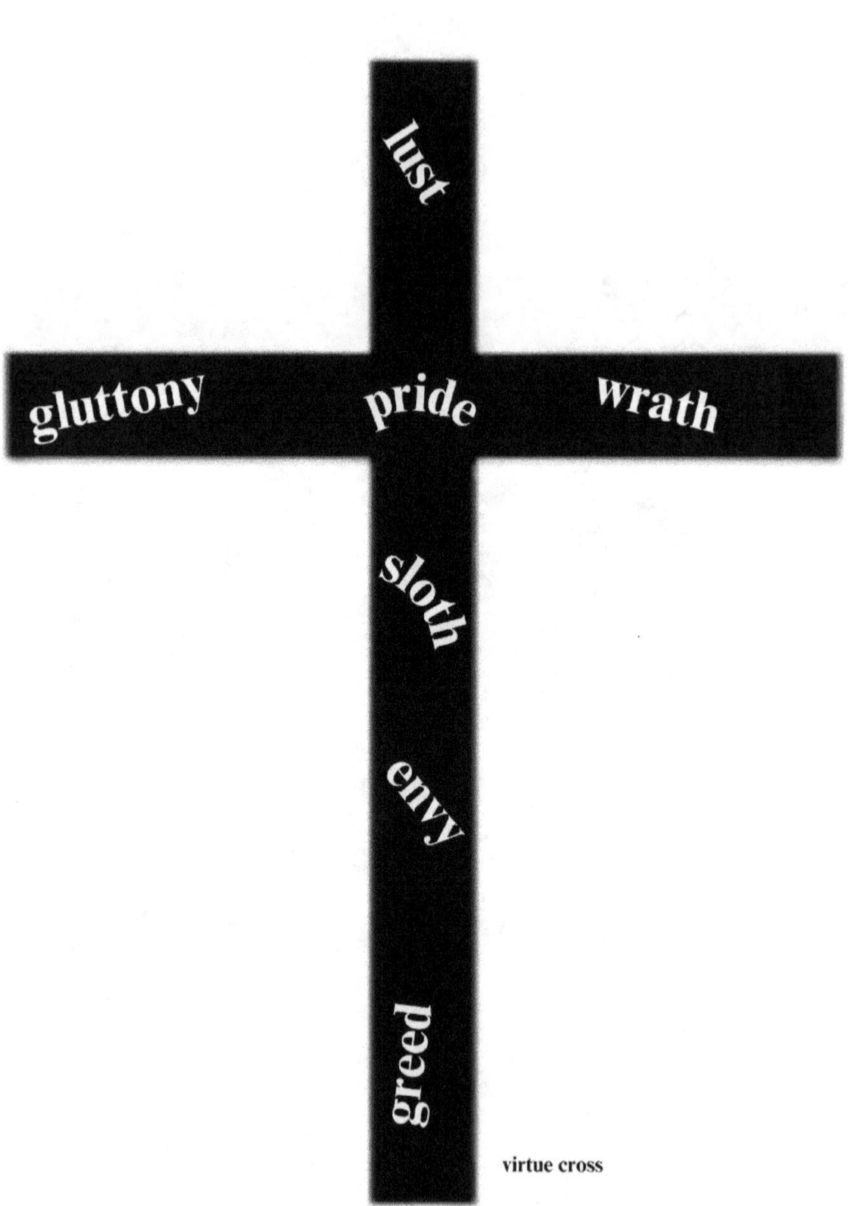

virtue cross

Minos' Intern

welcome to limbo
i'm ur hell sentencer
since the upgrade
i don't need your confession
i know ur deeds
u get me not Minos
no-one placed pennies on ur eyes
Charon is unpaid
he refused to cross u to hell
hell has warming 2
Styx is dry
i'll get 2 u

still making circle assignments by
the number of tail wraps
my tail is only a stub
can't wrap yet

ur deeds fit in2 many circles
place u in 1
familiar with ur sins? & the circles?
& how ur sins fit in2 circles?

i don't get hell topology
failed geography &
geometry 2 *
bad with where &
worse with shapes
let's begin

job sucks

dad made me

owe dad $

off 6 pm

get 2 6-packs Miller

betty's a slut

dairy qeen 1st

puck me up?

no car

c U 7

DOPE

temperance

kindness

diligence chastity humility

charity

patience

sin cross

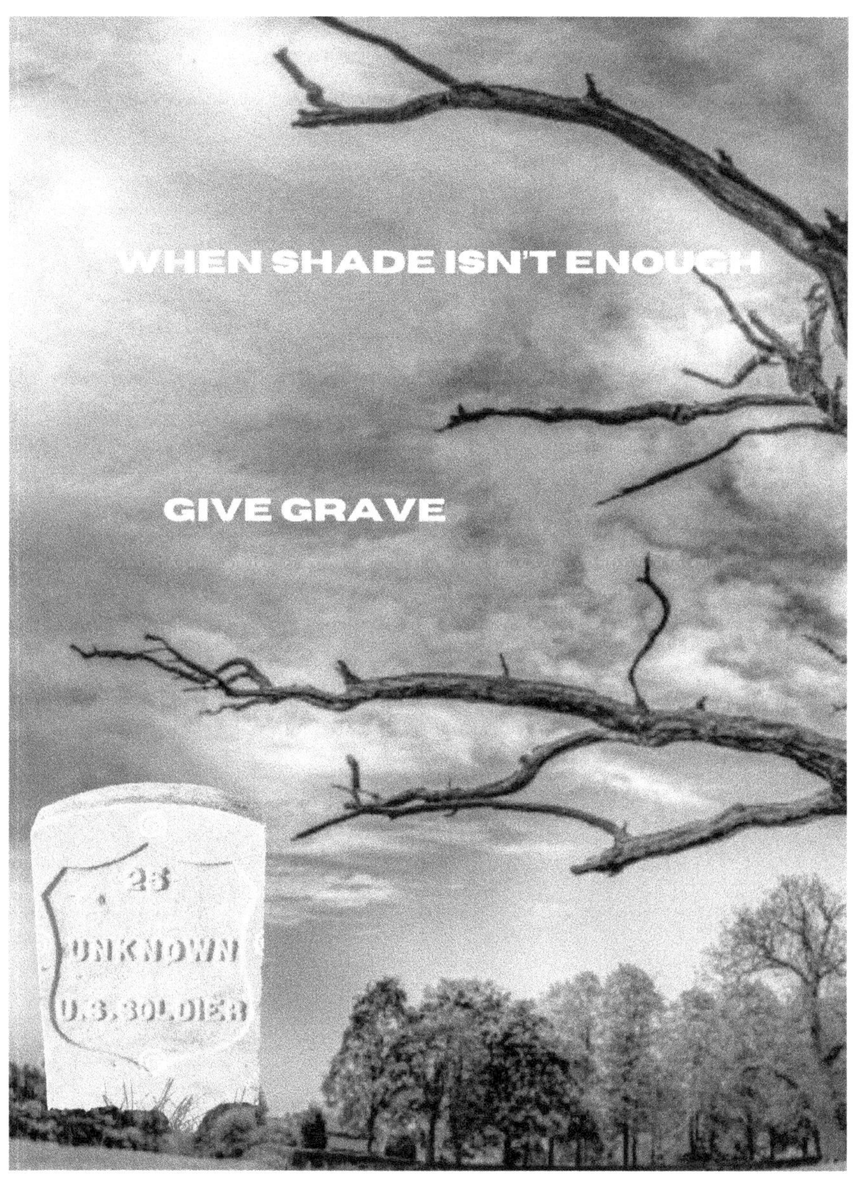
WHEN SHADE ISN'T ENOUGH
GIVE GRAVE
UNKNOWN
U.S. SOLDIER

Test of Fall

we are walking on a path toward each other
did you plant a GPS tracker in my butt?
how did you know I would fall into a ditch?
your bystander right hand reaches for my left hand

extend my hand?

Norman Bates was a character portrayed by Anthony Perkins in the movie *Psycho* filmed in the year 1960 at Universal Studios, Universal City Plaza, Universal City, CA 91608

December 11 Norman Bates Journal

Did
3 a.m. peed
6 a.m. hard wake up
poured out sour milk
ironed mother's dress
soaked sheets in Clorox
paid Fairvale CA property tax
sharpened knife

Saw/Noticed
corn-flakes stale
dusty Bates Motel sign
all rooms vacant
celery stuck in front tooth
hole in shower curtain
Marion's straight teeth
red hairs clog drain

Heard
radio alarm clock
key turns lock
silence
Marion scream
bathroom fan
shower water drains
siren

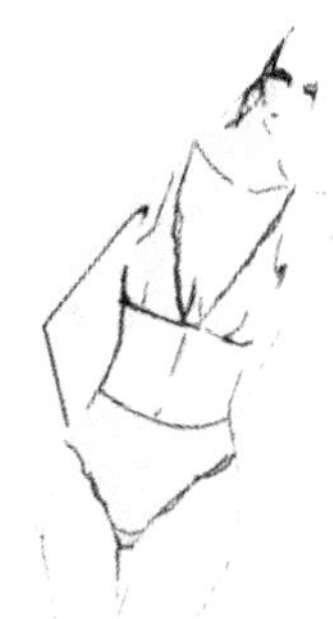

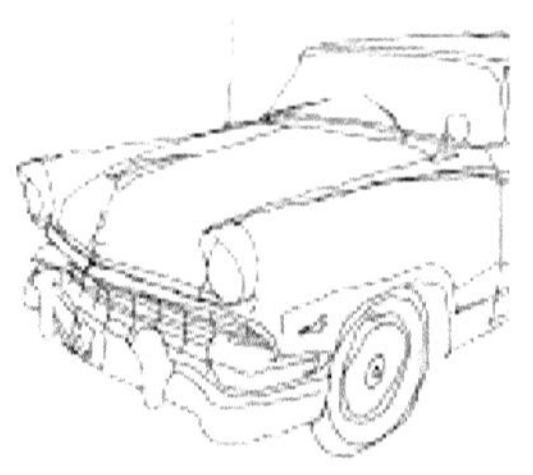

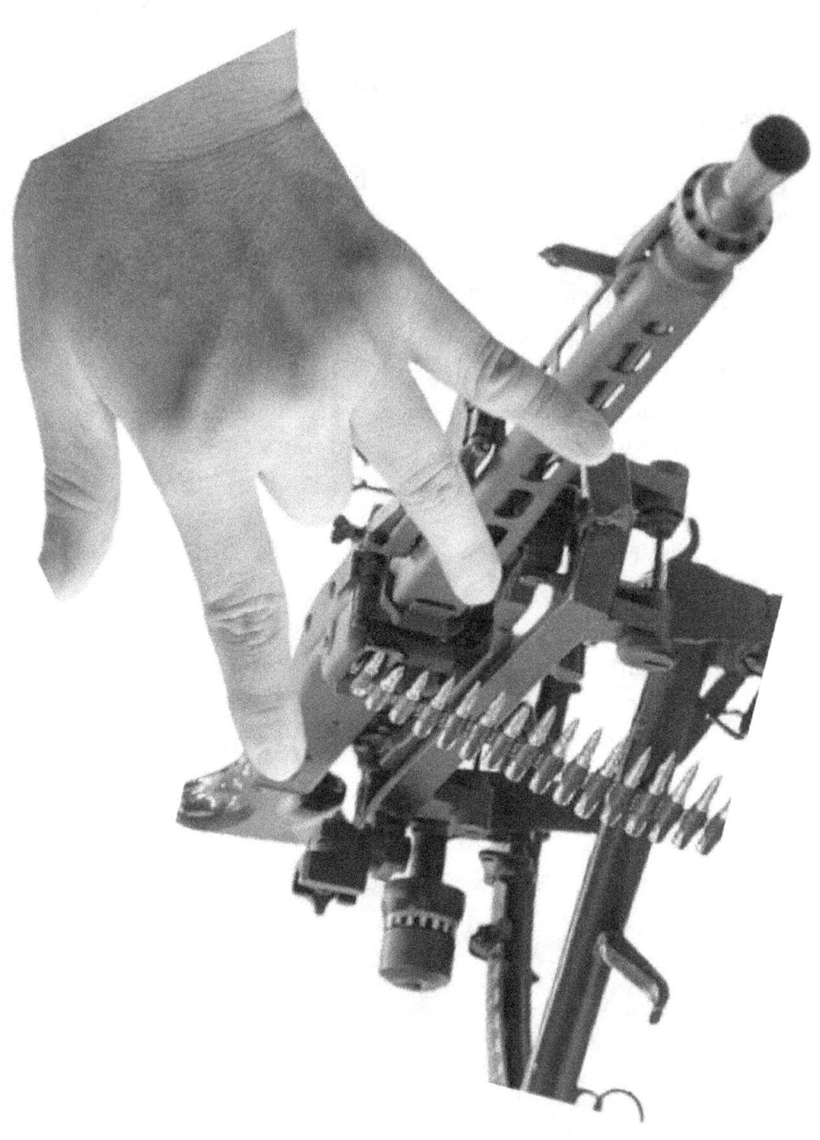

Trigger Finger Ends Gun Violence

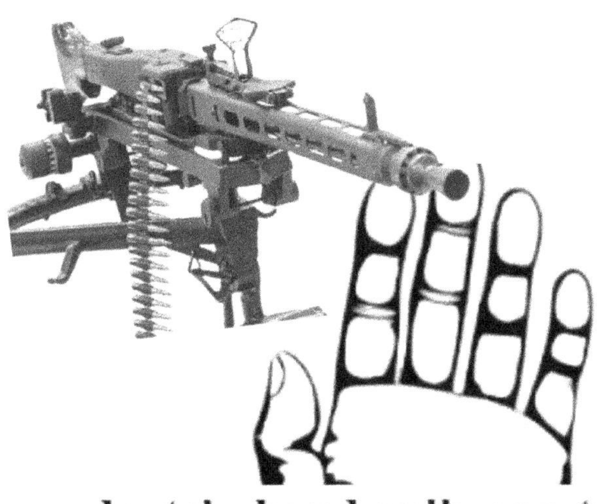

~~syndactyly~~ hand pulls gun trigger

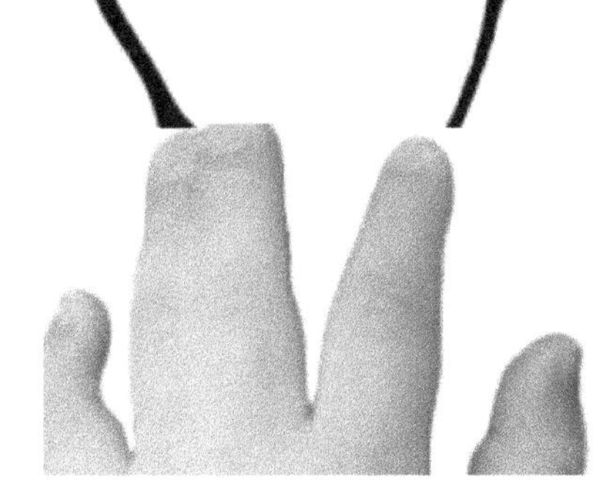

syndactyly hand ~~pulls gun trigger~~

syndactyly hand survives

survival of the fittest hand

Costello murders **Frankenstein**'s bride
Costello's Frankenstein's baby daddy
Abbott: *Costello it's me or Frank*

Abbott loves the **Mummy**
Costello uses the mummy as toilet paper
toilet paper prices sky rocket

WhereWolf's on 1st
Costello is a WhereWolf
Wherewolf lodge opens

Whose in the casket?
Abbott gives **Dracula** Hep-B
b-a-a-a-d blood

Publicist: all rumors are true
Frankenstein's baby 24 weeks early
Abbott's Costello's baby daddy

Abbott and Costello Monster Rumors

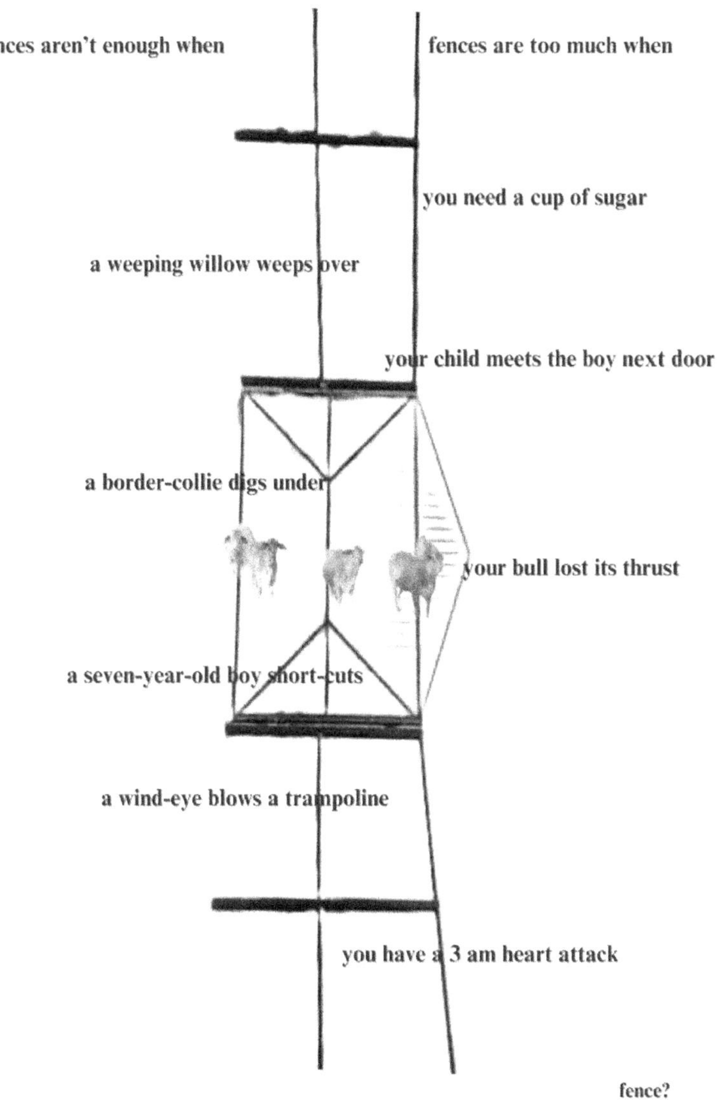
fences aren't enough when
fences are too much when
you need a cup of sugar
a weeping willow weeps over
your child meets the boy next door
a border-collie digs under
your bull lost its thrust
a seven-year-old boy short-cuts
a wind-eye blows a trampoline
you have a 3 am heart attack
fence?

United Nations finds pedestrian driver switch = peace

an ash quarter horse buggy buggies
& a Ford Model A four-wheeler
wheels over orange dust
& a red-seat Kawasaki
& silver side-car weaves between lanes

& Adam prams a pram
with two-month Jane
wailing

& Jill's hairless
right arm swings
a tan briefcase

& John jogger jogs in red striped
white sweat pants

> two-hundred years
pedestrians on the side
& vehicles in the center
~~more~~

the rules of the road Bill is law
roads will Bea gray cemented
& Olivia loads a Ford F-150
pick-up truck

& Jack's 33" haired legs
walk two-miles per hour
Nike step after Nike step

& Eve motors a white Ford F
wearing a black head-scarf
with tail tarring the sidewalk
cement

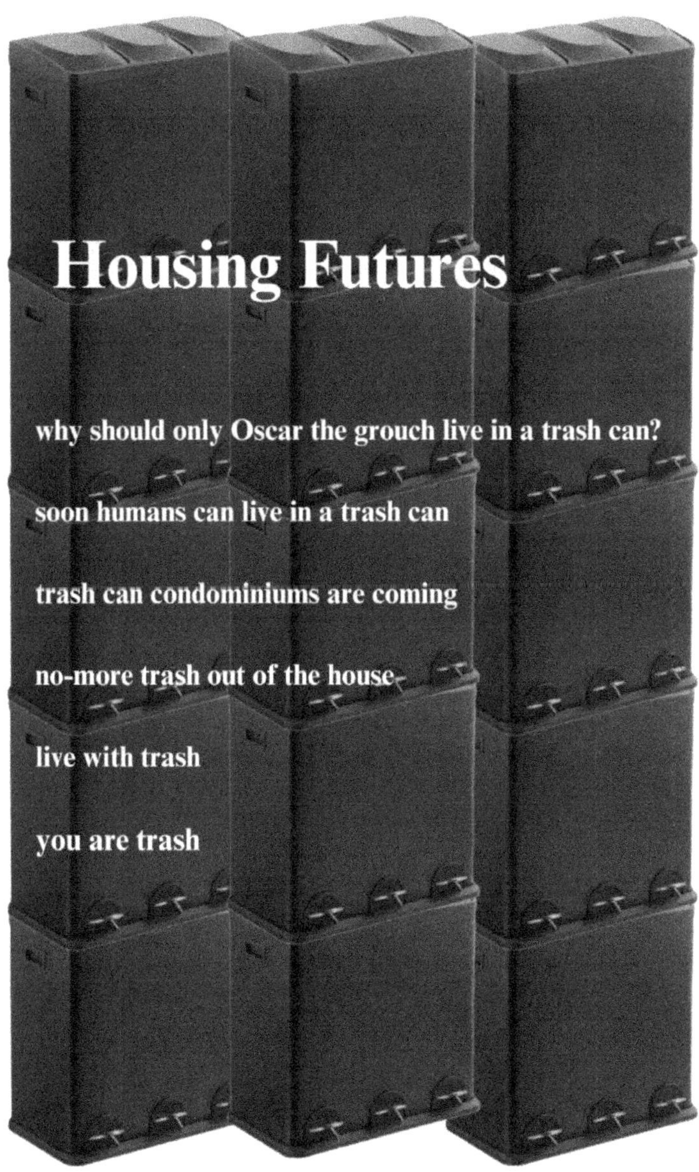

Housing Futures

why should only Oscar the grouch live in a trash can?

soon humans can live in a trash can

trash can condominiums are coming

no-more trash out of the house

live with trash

you are trash

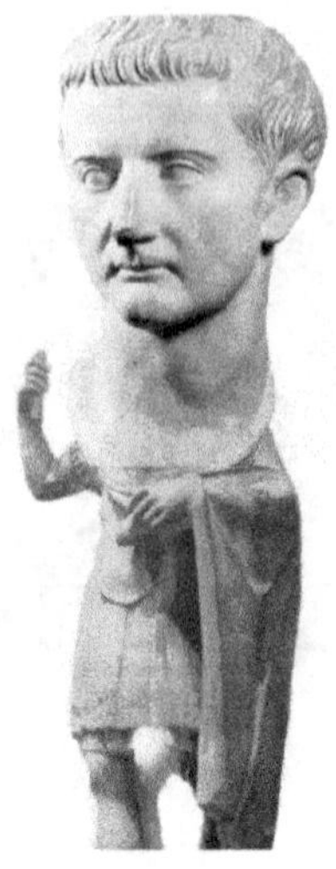

Tiberius
14–37 ad

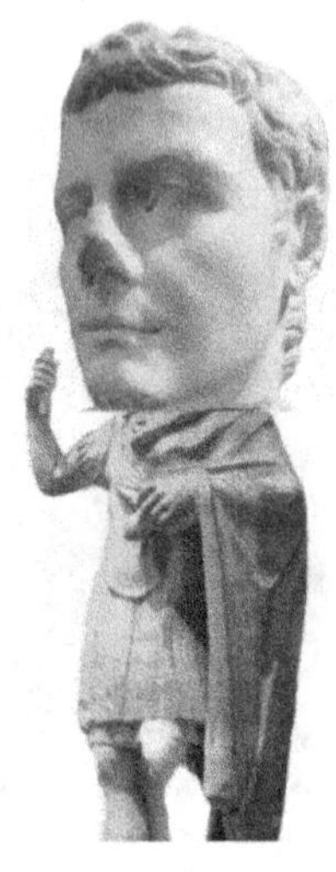

Caligula
37-41 ad

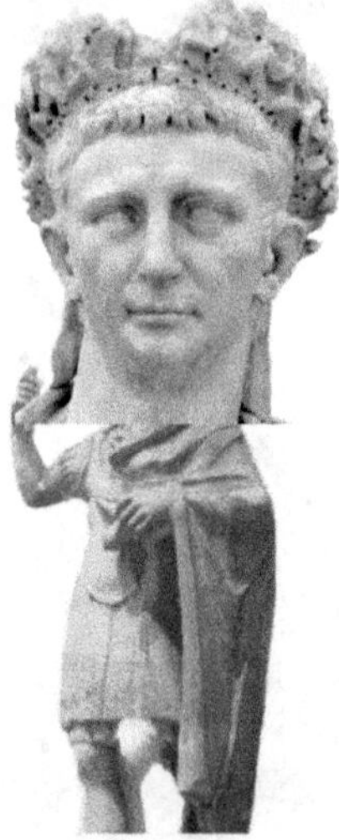

Claudius
41-54 ad

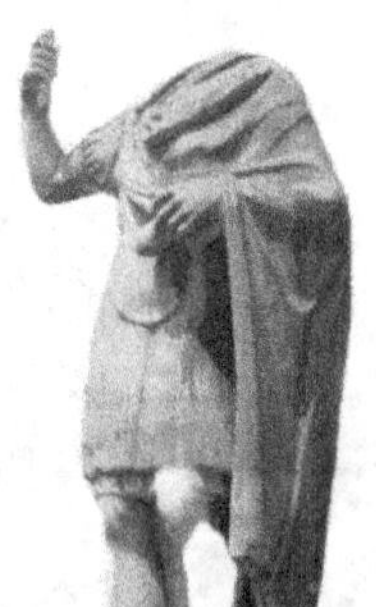

Roman Emporer statue succession planning

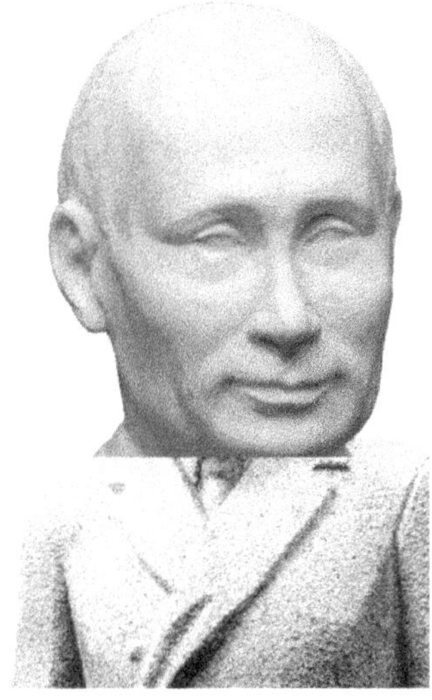

Vladimir Putin
2000-08

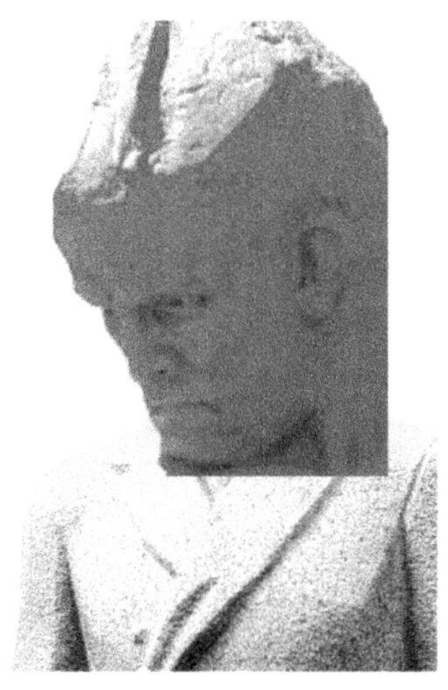

Dmitry Medvedev
2008-12

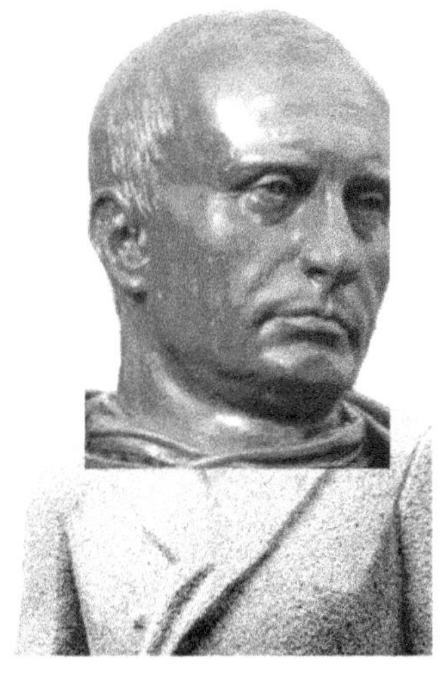

Vladimir Putin
2012-

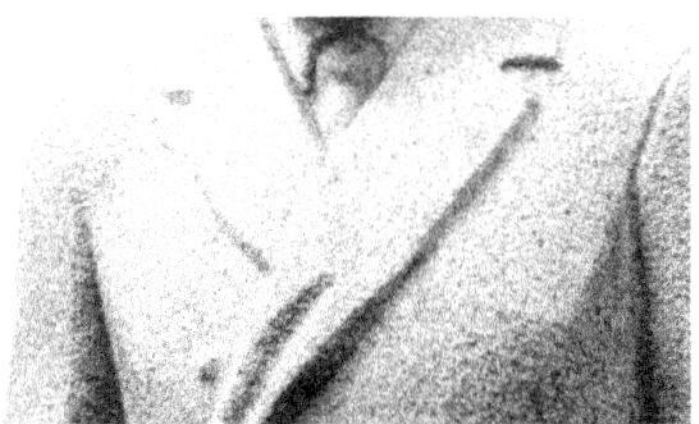

Russian President statue succession planning

ART
JST
PST
12
11
1
CST
STB
hour marker
band
tick
10
2
WIB
crystal
case
TOT
tim emit s a mit from t
tim 's ties his tie
tim et i, i et tim
it s t time 4 tim
t 'em tim emt s
9
hand
battery
3
LINT
CHADT
crown
dial
BST
8
pusher
bezel
lugs
4
ANAT
7
6
5
EST
LHST
AEST
IRST

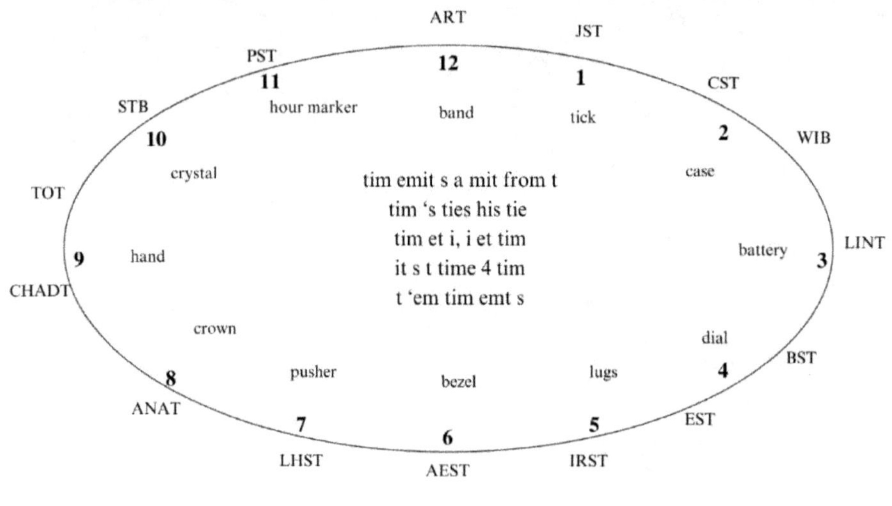

÷ time

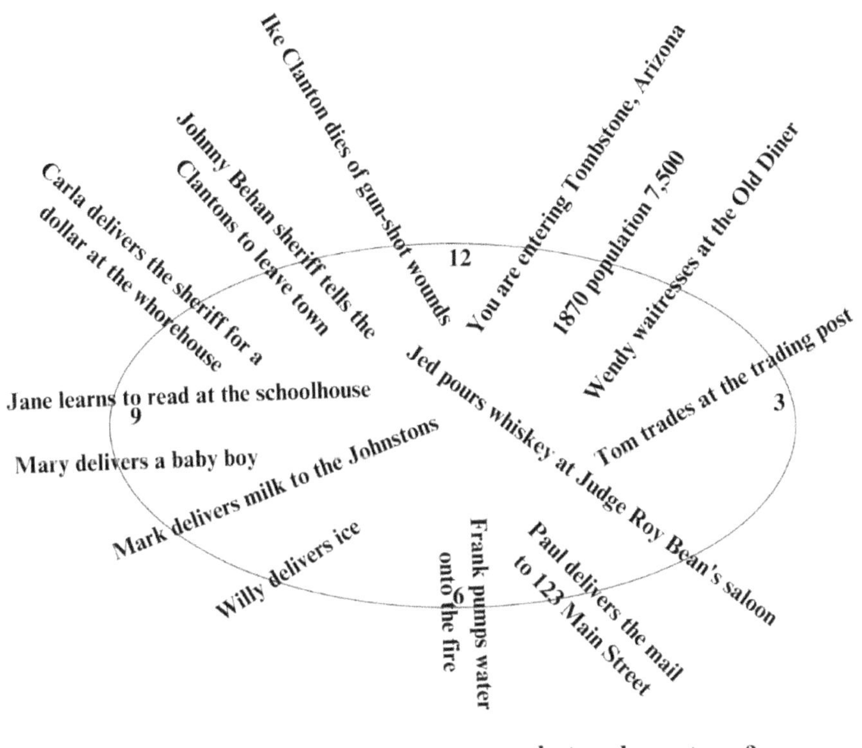

what makes a town?

patience only for my last line

**not enough servers to be served upon arrival
get in line**

**even if I self-check-out I wait for a scanner
cut in line**

**queue in the cafeteria for leftovers
bathroom line**

**race through the border at 90 m.p.h.
police chase line**

**will the doctor enter my room?
patient line**

**what happens at my death?
flatline**

white noir
robert fleming

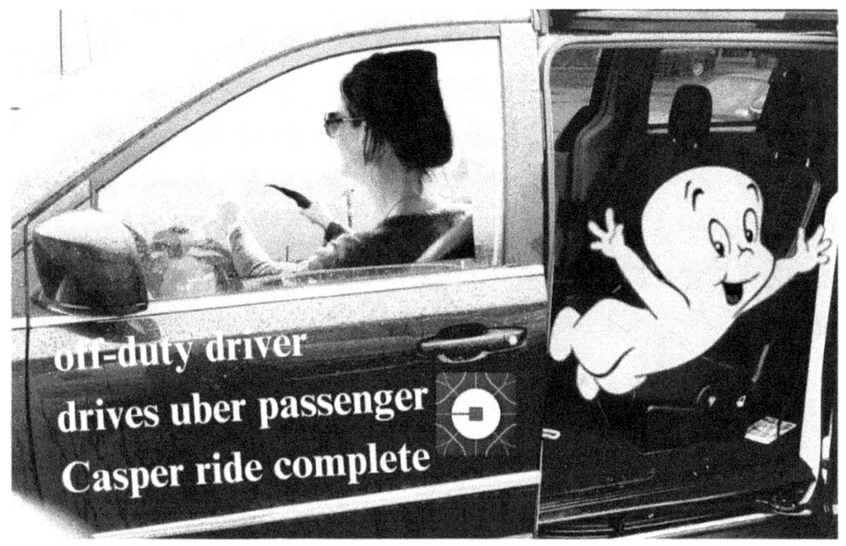

ALEXA

can miracles exist?

can I find love?
can I lose five pounds?
can I win the lottery?
can my run over coon hound be un-run?
can a wrung chicken neck be un-wrung?
can a decapitated head be recapped?
can the dead be resurrected?
can an ozone hole be filled?

no

another request?

five male singing voice grid

pretend	you're	a	bird	falsetto
highest	a	glass	breaks	countertenor
high	mountain	tops	snow	tenor
low	meadow	off	moss	baritone
lowest	sing	a	drum	bass

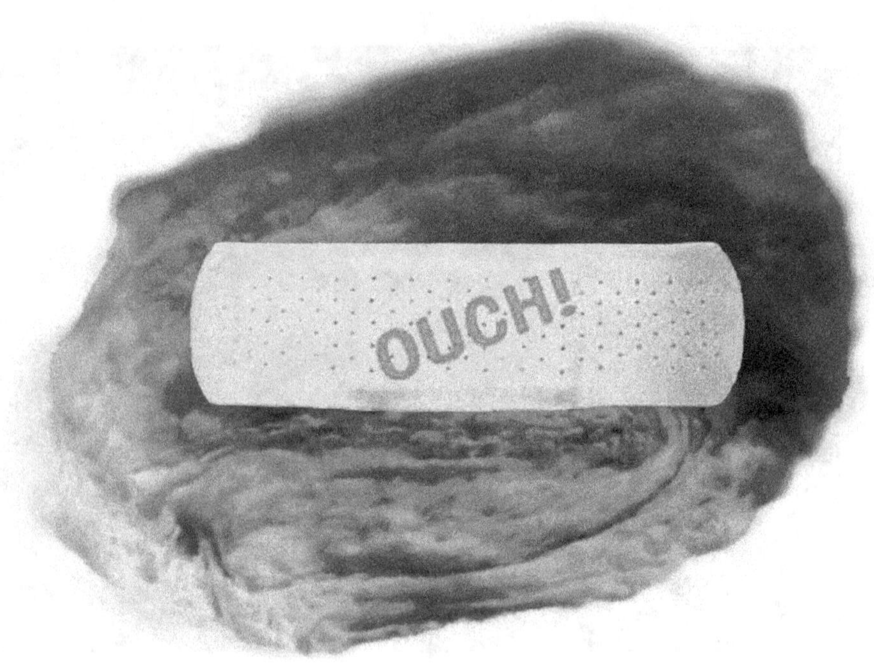

ozone repair trial #2001: band aid

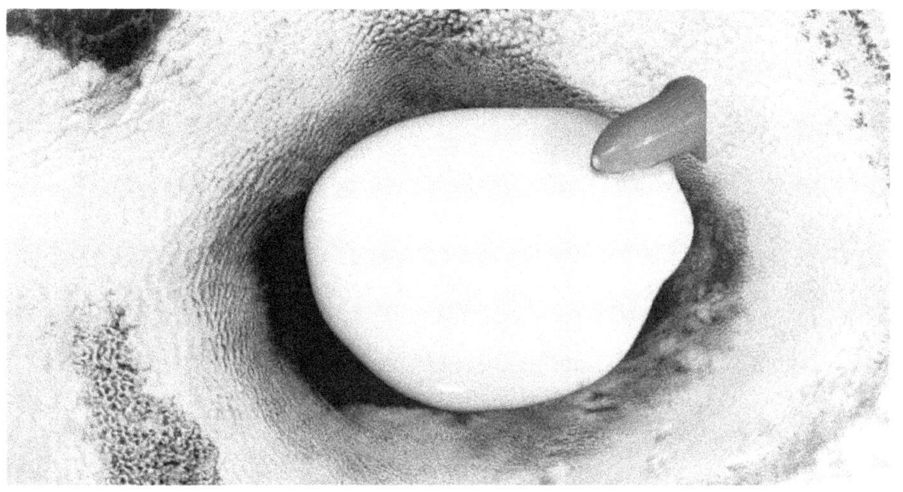

ozone repair trial #10022: Elmer's glue

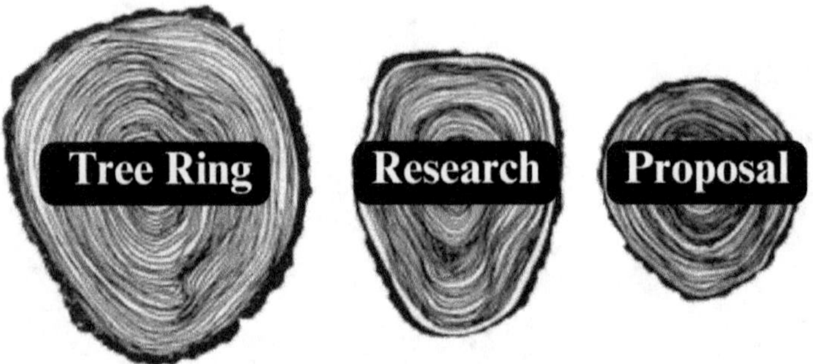

Background

Trees growing 25-65 degrees latitude form tree-rings. Andrew Douglass and Clark Wissler first dated tree-rings. Tree-ring color and width explain past climate. Global warming is measured by the trend in globally averaged temperature near the earth's surface.

Hypothesis: is a relationship between tree-rings and earth's temperature?

Method

sample: 100 logging trees in North America, Europe, and Asia
collect earth temperature from NASA Goddard
photograph, color matched, amd count tree-rings

Results

analysis: descriptive and inferential statistics
correlation between earth temperature and the number of tree trunk rings

Conclusion : estimate earth future life expectancy

white noir
robert fleming

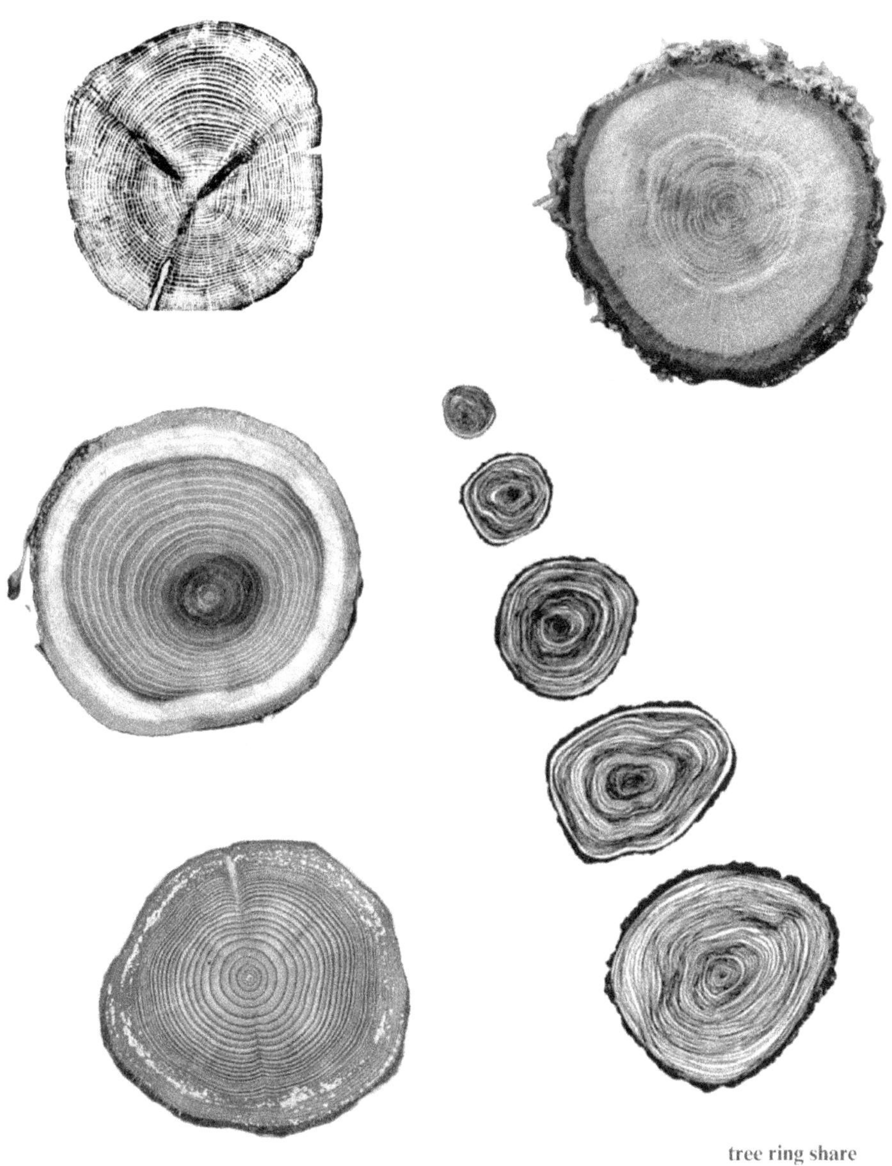

tree ring share

return to the garden

apple trees are under the sky but need a roof yks sdeen evE

pear trees are soiled but need a linoleum floor lios sdeen madA

cherry trees are in open space but need walls ecaps nepo sdeen kcaJ

banana trees have sap but need blood pas sdeen lliJ

move the orchard inside the house yks eht rednu snamuh lla nruter

we were before waring

we wore hair keratin like baboons &
knocked our chests like gorillas

we wore skin like zebras &
bent-over to water like wilder-beasts

we wore muscle like lions &
paw swatted flies like bears

we wore bones like swine &
dug dirt worms like robins

we wore blood like falcons &
taloned on branches like pigeons

we wore fig leaves like chameleons &
hide motionless like a rat out-preying an ambush snake

you named us Adam & Eve
we were before words

white noir
robert fleming

noir à blanche

white noir
robert fleming

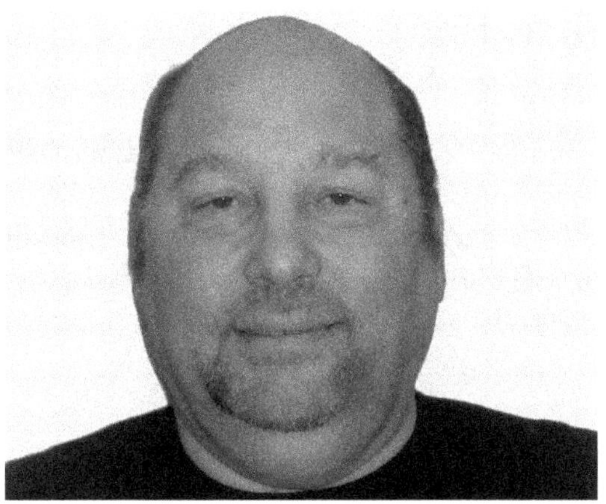

About the Author

Robert Fleming (b. 1963) is a visual-poet born in Montreal, Quebec, Canada who emigrated to Lewes, Delaware, United States. Robert follows his mother as a visual artist and his grandfather as a poet.

Robert knew noir before white. Growing up in Montreal, Quebec, he pointed at what he wanted, refusing to speak English. His mother sent him to French nursery school where his first word was *chat*, Cheryl, his sister's name.

As a child, Robert saw noir but was not afraid of the dark because he had a protector: a Star Trek night light. He also saw black by rubbing the bottoms of his feet in earth.

His first memory of white was chasing Penny, his German-Shephard, in a one-piece yellow snow-suit until his inside suit was filled with snow. At Westmount's Muray-Hill park, he was one-of-ten kids at the bottom of the toboggan slope in a kid pile.

A new color, blue, dictated his first creation of visual poetry: a grade-six French notebook.

After his retirement in 2018, Robert continued creating visual poetry. His themes are masculinity, sexual orientation, sin and virtue, and dystopia. His style is experimental on the edge influenced by the writers Robert Frost, Dr. Seuss, and the Beats and his graphics by surrealistic artists like Salvador Dali. More than 500 of his works were published internationally in more than 100 print and online publications, art galleries and open mic features. He is a featured or repeat contributor to Devil's Party Press, Mad Swirl, Medusa's Kitchen, Synchronized Chaos, California Quarterly, Four Feathers Press, and Spectrum.

He does service for writers as a founding and contributing editor of Old Scratch Press. He is also a member of the Rehoboth Beach Writer's Association and Horror Writers Association.

Robert is an award winner: 2023 shortlisted for Blood Rag poet of the year; 2022 Delaware Press Association: 2 honorable mentions; 2022 San Gabriel Valley California Broadside-1 poem, 2021 Best of Mad Swirl poetry; Nominations: 2 Pushcart and 2 Best of the Net.

Robert is always collecting new images for work. If someone is stalking graphic images on Google, it's Robert.

Follow Robert: facebook.com/robert.fleming.5030

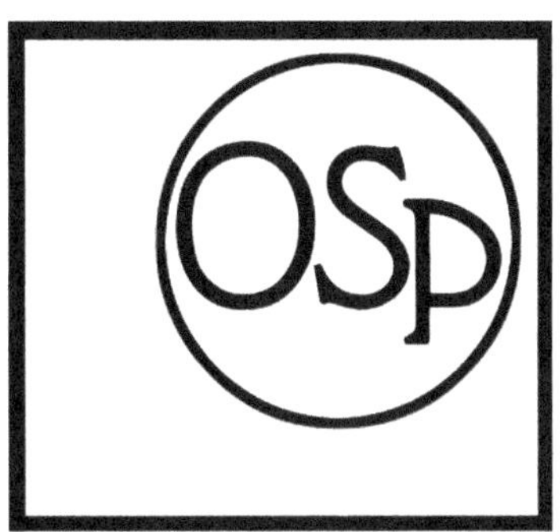

Founded in 2023, Old Scratch Press is a
cooperative of poets and short-form authors
who have come together to promote the
publication and appreciation of poetry
and short-form writing.
Robert Fleming's **white noir** is the second book
from this endeavor. We hope you've enjoyed it.

oldscratchpress.com

www.ingramcontent.com/pod-product-compliance
Lightning Source LLC
LaVergne TN
LVHW010943110826
845149LV00013B/2737

* 9 7 8 1 9 5 7 2 2 4 1 8 3 *